To
Put
The
Mouth
To

The National Poetry Series

The National Poetry Series was established in 1978 to ensure the publication of five books of poetry each year through a series of participating publishers. Each manuscript is selected by a poet of national reputation. Publication is funded by the Copernicus Society of America, James A. Michener, Edward J. Piszek, and The Lannan Foundation.

1991 Publications

Good Hope Road by Stuart Dischell
Selected by Thomas Lux. Viking / Penguin

The Dig by Lynn Emanuel
Selected by Gerald Stern. University of Illinois Press

To Put The Mouth To by Judith Hall
Selected by Richard Howard. William Morrow and Company, Inc.

As If by James Richardson
Selected by Amy Clampitt. Persea Books

A Flower Whose Name I Do Not Know by David Romtvedt
Selected by John Haines. Copper Canyon Press

To
Put
The
Mouth
To

JUDITH HALL

WILLIAM MORROW AND COMPANY, INC.
NEW YORK

This collection is dedicated to
Alec Bernstein

It is the policy of William Morrow and Company, Inc., and its imprints and affiliates, recognizing the importance of preserving what has been written, to print the books we publish on acid-free paper, and we exert our best efforts to that end.

Library of Congress Cataloging-in-Publication Data

Hall, Judith, 1951–
    To put the mouth to / Judith Hall.
        p.   cm.
    Includes bibliographical references.
    ISBN 0-688-11547-0
    I. Title.
  PS3558.A3695T6   1992b
  811′.54—dc20   91-35307
                                                                          CIP

Printed in the United States of America

First Edition

1 2 3 4 5 6 7 8 9 10

BOOK DESIGN BY NICOLA MAZZELLA

Acknowledgments

Grateful acknowledgment is made to the editors of the following publications in which these poems first appeared: *Boulevard,* "Song of Many Pauses"; *The Cooke Book* (SCOP), "Taboo"; *The Kenyon Review* (Winter 1992), "In an Empty Garden"; *The New Republic,* "A Letter," "Postcard of Degas' *Washerwomen Carrying Washing";* *Shenandoah: The Washington and Lee University Review,* Fragments of an Eve: Scraps from Her Album— "Fragments of an Eve," "Her Plainsong," "Pictures of an Exhibition"; *Western Humanities Review,* "Robes," "A Wild Plum Is for Independence."

I would like to thank the Ingram Merrill Foundation and the Maryland State Arts Council for grants of financial assistance and the MacDowell Colony and the Corporation of Yaddo, where a number of these poems were composed.

I would also like to thank Richard Howard, David St. John, and Michael Glaser for critical support.

Tell me where dwell the thoughts
forgotten till thou call them forth?
William Blake

Contents

Fragments
of an Eve:
Scraps from
Her Album

Untitled

Come, wake, encumber the skull
Of the one who makes signs for water,
Not knowing them. Rain comes,
Delicious for the assembled dawn,
The dawn redwood: discovered again
After having long been considered extinct.
Me too. I was not supposed to see this.
I cup my hands, pink flames, to drink.

Fragments of an Eve

II

At first, I could not see past *that*—that
Shivering green flared around bits too bright
For color. I had nothing to say—shy,
Perhaps, or nauseous from the perfumed blasts
Of simple shapes above. He said I had
No memory, but when I had, my mind
Would settle into a slower pace—a "time
For Dusk-Dark-Dawn-Days-That-Pass."

And though he held me till the colors turned
Into each other—(slowly, a sleeping blue
Became the unimpeded nothing, black,
And then, as slowly, gray chirped and bloomed)—
I was back beneath the churning din,
Not what he said, "alive"; only afraid.

III

Crickets rubbing vowels across the iris-
Colored air, vowels swivel through laughter. "You
Dreamed her." Is this another of Father's jokes?
They laugh together: sounds still improvised.
A laugh not quite a word, a *why*
Broken into pieces, repeated: *Who; who*
Rehearsals: h, hă, hē, hŏo—how one
Sound leaves the sucking litter, climbing

Up into his lap: Look at me!
A babble of eyes, or are they fireflies?
He smiles the way his father smiles.
Are crickets laughing too? "She dreams of dancing
With an old white man." But I am not laughing.
Do not. Please do not dream for me.

Landscape Instead of Prayer

Shark eye moon shell, for instance,
    Is hurled at sand:
        Shallow lavender

Gray taken back and back: ebb
    Lip. Then more stars buffeting
        Sponges, flung mussels,

Conches; bluish crash.
    Hinged wings, once curved, split; purples
        Splinter; lightning whelks.

They shine in water–
    Light, where the water fondles
        Anything: sea glasses, o–

Vals of amber, emerald,
    Indigo, pounded
        Under bubbles and

Ribbons of eelgrass. And there,
    No one cares what fades,
        What fails to resemble us.

IV

I lift against his skin; he lifts me up.
And I rub his skin like rubbing the air for food.
Again he lifts me up, skin to the curve
Of skin. In dreams, touching is not enough.
And he rubs me on his skin, rubs me under—
"Wake up," he says. Then I—; then he—; but
Do I know what I want? His hands under
My arms, lifting me up? I want—what?

Another dream of his hush upon
Mine; mine, his? And wake, and what is gone:
Mouths kissing husks of hush. And dreams
Of holy hands, rubbing innuendos
Of my body in his day. Are words dreams
Of one refrain: *I am alone. Where are you?*

VI

"How did it happen?" he asks; the grass
Unflattens as he turns. The shadows handle
Grass, a repetition of his hands
In breath-entangled hair, and I am heated
Under words like *animal, sister, his.*
Possessives fix and hiss the world into
His echo: Nothing like a music that is
His. I push his words together, believing

They are mine: *Bluegrass. Buffalo grass.*
But are these his too, scratching
My mouth to shadows? At least his hands
Lead along the lip of *tell me,*
Along the rib of *hold me,*
Along the //, the calligraphic weeds, the *we.*

VIII

Am I happy—*hap*—*chance*—a random
"Passion," a variant of touching,
He said. Am I happy if only lucky,
Only happened to be here, apprehended
From a bone? He called a rib my ancestor,
By which I thought he meant a joke, a pun
On how I tickle him. Instead, he grinned,
Pointing low, where his chest began to shadow

On the stomach. What could I reply,
Running through grass to the shore, where light
Scarred the water gray, a color like a
Clam hugged by starfish, like a
Reprimand, as if I have no faith,
And prayer were only crossing my fingers for praise.

Her Plainsong

We eat all day and by aroma—pears,
Almonds, olives. We find enough to eat.
And happy when we do not think about it,

When we laugh about our feasts: Who found
The most mushrooms; who found the wild ginger.
We eat all day and by aroma. Pears

Fill up our hands. And then we do not touch
Each other, busy with our teeth, busy mouths.
And happy when we do not think about it.

Laughing like the black that pecks the core
Of pears—seeds like silence, like forgetting.
We eat all day and by aroma: pear-

Liquid on chins. Ideas parallel and may
Refrain; happy when we think alike.
And happy when we do not think about it.

We forget then and then and then,
What happens beyond our own amusement.
We eat all day and by aroma—pears,
Apples, happy when we do not think about it.

XVI

If I built a lover from my father's clay,
Chiseling a younger version of features
Memorized, would I, later, seem
A lunatic, too bothered by archaic
Idols, worship; a woman in heat for a savior?
If I built a lover, he would study Greek,
Pluck apple blossoms, handfuls wreathing
My hair, and would he be my father? A vague

Approximation of what I want, what I remember.
If I built a lover from my father's clay,
I would be caught between what I forget—
How he smelled when he approached—and phrases
He repeated—*someone will take care of you*—
As if he never gave me solitude.

XXVII

Before I go to him tonight, and I will,
I want a better skin, more like the bark
On apple trees, abrasive, rooted armor,
Where scabs layer, knotted to a crust, a solid
Skin, padded with brittle leaves, thickening
Plate with husk, scales, caked and gnarled
In stiffened scowls, scars, practiced hard,
A harder surface for his reprimand.

Or has he missed me? Will he ask me to lie
With him, the way we—the way leaves matted
Under us and slid? Memories rob
The world of its restraint, and we fracture
On what was and what was not resolved,
Imagined. Skin, all fingernails for a while.

XXVIII

And I would fall in him—and introduce
Him to a throat erupting—what a tongue
Could do. The waking we let each other
Do. I miss him, miss the murmur crooned
When all around us, the river nuzzles with moon-
Light the blue herons and crabs. Such advantages
To adoration—"to put the mouth to." Voluptuous
Touches—no one body or two—no one way to

Touch. Then would I be stuck in these embraces—
Afraid again—as if the world replaced
Itself with kisses and ran off. Love
Is difficult when not reduced to pulses
Sucking. A love awake, of words and hands—
How flesh meets flesh through rinds of I am, I am.

Pictures of an Exhibition

Look at me.
Pornography is easier in black and white.
The gray breasts surprise less than flesh.

I learn to look back at the camera; my smile, timed.
Only if I were art would I avert my eyes.
He said, "We will clip your pubic hair.

Here and there.
That much darkness makes a hole on paper."
He praised my body, the way I lean on my shadow,
    obedient.

The way he rinsed the negatives to this:
Beauty spots along the back; coloring, grisaille.
Look closer till you do not seem alone.

Yes, I made myself an image.
You saw the raw light along a shoulder sink in thighs.
Do not idealize.

Or admit how long ago, how often.
One image twists the others to a single shape.
Then ellipsis, what I may erase.

Lines are only two shades meeting.
My father saw a little girl, a picture every gesture.
Is more narration needed?

He loved me with his camera until the looking came
    between.
I was afraid of so much watching
As though I were a memory he needed.

He saw my bath, the bubbles patterning my back.
The laugh is half a licking of my lips.
I am five: He loves me with his camera.

And words fall off from exhibition.
And I would faint in such desire.
Or vomit, tear myself apart the way he looks at me.

He holds me and I know his silhouette.
Afraid to press him back.
I wanted a bed with bars, cutting the land beyond

Blankets into simpler shapes,
Holding me in when I roll at night.
No shapes approach without asking first.

I will be alone. Some images work alone.
Crosses on the wall, flung by carlight,
Seem a crossing out of hours.

If this happened long ago, you would know
I was the one accusing him of loving me
Like a god. I wanted a god.

The nudity of sacred figures we approve.
My mother said, "Your father would do anything for
 you."
Look at me. You cannot see enough.

Taboo

I take into silence my silence—what
I will not say,
Watching white leaves in sunlight wave.
I tell myself,
I forgot what I would say. And birds
Flit by; their dark
Flashes dart along the old imprinting.
Green odors
Wake and turn. If I approach those wishes,
They talk back
From hiding places—worms emerging
After rain—
And so I sleep, afraid, small again, as I
Would be outside.
Sleep protects the way a window tells you
What to see:
The leaves, more yellow in the moving light.
Sleep tucks sound
Away. "Don't frown when you think,"
My mother said.
She came in with laundry. "Don't frown.
You'll wrinkle your skin."
Sleep helps in simple erasures, though what if
I remember
When the rain stopped and children played
Near rhododendron;
Oklahoma. Honeysuckle
Reached the windows,
And when my father watered vines, honey rinsed
The air again.

Perhaps it was then that I became silent
With my father.
I was six and watched from the porch as he
Let the water
Fall over petals and into the little straws
I always slipped
Out, touching honey on my tongue. He smiled
At me, but words—
What word first? And even now, when my father
Holds me, though he
Ages into white and blue, even now, well—
He whispers over
The tablecloth as Mother stacks
Dishes in the kitchen.
"You are like me," he says. "You dream."
Then Mother enters,
Balancing plates and forks, the leftover cake, what
The neighbors say.
"Did you notice the new fence? The birds did."
My father nods.
He looks at me. Through the window, birds call out,
In danger or mating.
If I knew what I heard, I would know what to say.

XXXIII

I try not to think
how dead the trees look in winter:
cold puckers of skin,
twisted and stuck. And stillness,
a reprimand
of hurrying, as if
I saw pollen blossom perfume into
dust in minutes.

And the day
stuffs itself back
into blue. Words:
"tomorrow." "Years"—and I collapse
into the chatter birds
Prefer: *I. I love. Who comes. Danger.*

In an Empty Garden

Better to fall, better to fall than wait
To be held in air; wanting to be held,
Held in words we use when we embrace.
I wanted to be held in air or fall,

To be held in air. Wanting to be held,
I fell along the air's slow drawl,
Wanting to be held in air or fall,
As the turning of a body turned a voice away.

I fell along the air's slow drawl,
Away from words *abundance, blame,*
As he turned his body, turned his voice away,
As if I shed the words and gave them shape.

The word *abundance,* the word *blame:*
I handed him a place to put his tongue
And shed the words and gave them shape:
A snake, turning his skin into a skeleton.

I handed him a place to put his tongue,
A place where we knew why we kissed.
Like a snake, turning his skin into a skeleton,
I turned the air to kisses, golden nipples,

Any place. I knew why we kissed.
Another apple, another, another tongue.
The air will turn to kisses, golden nipples.
He wanted me to say I did it: Touched

Another apple, another, another tongue.
I will not tell you what we whispered.

He wanted me to say I did it, touched
A history of wishes to be held.

I will not tell you what we whispered.
I wanted him to help me question
A history of wishes: to be held,
Waiting, again, for that first kiss.

Help me. Help me question
The words we use when we embrace,
Waiting again for that first kiss—
Better to fall, better to fall than wait.

XXXVI

        Monday: Momentary snow:
The blue spires of juniper, pine
Pocked white:
        : Waiting: Shouldn't I
Wait: For the chill to give this cluttered
Wind a shape: Like white tongues:
     : Once rocks, roads: Cloud-color:
       : Dig an H for *Hello:*

      or hurt: or   the echo of hurt:
Ha ha: : So I spin: Abridged dances:
   : My body: Pearled in ice: Bead-whorls
       of hail singing in hair:
As if I believe the dream that brags:
You can do anything: Enter the world:

A Fluency in
Blame

A Fluency in Blame

Who could she blame now; or no,
Not now; no matter when,
It was the same language: a fluency
In blame: from *blasphēmāre,*

Reproach; a word "continuously popular"
And multipurpose. So when in doubt,
She turns to blame, repeating,
"Lamborghini," "Mitsubishi,"

For warming a white and humid sky.
The beauty of her blame:
A gestural idiom anyone could learn
Through repetition. Who could she blame

For the beauty of mahogany,
Carved ivory. Who took it away?
Who needed it more?
Soon other voices came to loving blame

The way she did: the beauty of a bench
Aging silver in the rain; the teak,
Ringed in summer bellflowers.
Anyone could blame the Javanese

For the inadvertent beauty
Of what remains, available, *ailanthus,*
Ghetto palms, "The Tree of Heaven."
Who could she blame
Or blame for the love of blame? The love of Camels

And Lucky Strikes. And "Honey,
Have you got a light?"
"What I love is my wife, my son, and my sailboat."

Words that are available work anyway.
"Do you know what I mean?"
Predictable gestures of affection
Without apologies:

Send roses, the red sweethearts.
Or send a collage, the last chance
For music, after "beauty is no longer available,
After Hiroshima, Agent Orange,"

(As if she remembered, as if she needed
Some change from suffering to the tune of—)
Primitive little prayer-noises.
Sorry. Sorry for all that happened.

Say it again, touching the marble hem of his garment.
Something to do with her hands:
The formal approach to blame.
So nice to find the right word,

As if she could walk away,
Not to blame. No one is to blame.
Times change, as when she walked away
To buy tuna. Buy grapes.
Wasn't it easier when there were action words
For blame, like mustard gas, grenade?

The war that was a poem by Rupert Brooke.
Remember action words for beauty:

Penicillin, Shirley Temple, Waring Blendor,
Even if millions of viewers already knew
The times could change again.
And anyone could tell her—and would, soon—

That she forgot to blame someone
For drunk drivers, hamburgers, alligator bags.
Anyone could blame her
For all the times she never made

America happy, and still assumed that she
Could say the right—, the word
That would cure, and happily ever after,
No questions asked.

Refrains:
Be Still

Dear Reader,

This will never change—
This asking, "What happened next?"

She read, "the slow arrangements on old albums
Enclose a room in a voice like sauterne.

And she would finger spotted petals—"
Remember what happened when she turned

The page? "The lilies he gave her scented her hands."
How much will the world decorate

The day's imaginings?
How much will the brain turn away?

Day after day, she waited for a bus, returning
To the time "when they lay, shadowed under lilies."

But the world—the world as work.
The world as attack and broadcast every day,

Unless she turned away, her eyes fixed on
Paperbacks: "Later, more laughter

Cuddled under wool. A lullaby of kisses—"
The world was never too much with her,

But a ghost nodding, later, on the evening news.
Cut that part, unless you want

To read it as a time when the world
Turned on itself, like the heroine,

Turning her days into shadows for romance,
Her days, half-erased, like memories

Improved. And you, Reader, know
When she waits for the bus—or when "I"—

When I ride to work before I'm awake,
I dream away the street, the amber bottles,

Plastic knives, and dream that I'd do more,
Awake, than read, "he asked her—"

And actually care, turning faster to the part
Where "streets, saturated by the twilit rain,

Made them laugh, even the litter," last chapter,
And I look up. The roughened trees

Lift their leaves above the traffic.
Not a metaphor, yet, of a woman lifting

Hair off her neck, watching him watch her.
Read her. Let herself be won like that and wanted.

A woman's pornography: Romance,
With fatigue as an excuse to keep on reading,

"He asked her, kneeling, bringing calla lilies,
And the world included her answer."

Her Epithalamium

I hesitate here at the beginning,
Though this should be the easy part,
Cushioned in momentary luxury:

The fragrances of lilies idling with
Roses, while I am powdered, curled,
Entranced in lace, in the little shapes where skin

Shows. I watch the obbligato
Décolletage, embellished now by women
Pressing rouge against my chest.

The whiter powder makes me laugh; its perfumed
Dust festooned with ancient veils,
Flame-colored marvels like prehensile tails.

A wedding hails the woman for a moment,
Her "only moment," worshipped by guests
Who raise their alabaster-colored beverages,

Waving gifts of falcons, alligator masks.
She knows this is the only goddess
Opportunity, and soon she will pass

From man to man. But do not think of that,
As he stands, waiting near the aisle.
Remember running, running handsprings,

Rolling down hills of violets, fields, pinks,
Eating lemon marigold.
And wishes for wings or fins,

Wishing herself foam, as the flutes begin:
Let everyone stand,
As Father and I walk the hall in candlelight.

Was what I knew a dream, before
The watered white brocaded silk and hours
Choosing shoes? To prove I am not alone, or—

"Wilt thou—wilt thou depart?" Leaving me
To learn the touch of another family,
Another couple. The fear of couples:

Who will lead and who will pay and love.
Love—a laxative for the heart:
Giving knitted mufflers, giving oval

Tins of divinity—until "They two shall be
One flesh." No one could say that again!
To walk so far, only to be back in the body

Of another, saying, "I will. I will fall back
Into one flesh, looking up, my mouth
Open, waiting." But do not think of that.

Remember "love": "It delights: *Gilouban;*
Geliefan; beleven; believe. We *believe* in what we *love,*
Though to *leave* is part of its history."

I know how to leave, looking back, afraid
Of "gathering together." Laughing alone, I—
Anger is the part, washed in champagne,

That returns as laughter. So laugh that I would leave
A love that may be more than a begging for someone
To hold. Please turn now to a litany

Of the hors d'oeuvres. Descriptions fix
On the present, on abundance, without quite
The vulgarity of ecstasy.

(So try the peppers stuffed with pepper
Chèvre, the shrimp, the *baba ganouj,* or salad.)
Please let it be easy to forget,

So we may walk out, startled, into the lilac–
Shadowed square, as Father waves,
Smiling, waves and turns away.

Postcard of Degas'
Washerwomen Carrying Washing

They both lean away from smudged yellow,
Burnt sienna; their baskets heaped with pillows,
Pillow-heaps. The washerwomen's hips
(The skirted, aproned, muslin, gray) help
Them carry folded wash. Looking down,
Smeared with chalk, a scumble of glue,
They look where they are going and lean at you.

Dear A., If you were here, you'd laugh at all
The roaches in the Brite-Wash, touching crusted
Soap in empty washers. And drunks trudge in,
(You wouldn't laugh, but would you help?)
  coughing
Under smokey steam by the windows, talking
A kind of drawled homage to "a wonderful
Ohio," while women drink Coke and huddle
Away, smoothing warm shirts on hangers:
Their hands on husband ghosts and other ghosts,
Themselves: their hosiery and finery.
Winter colors, silver, white. They borrow
Soap. I don't need to help, don't need
To say anything, but if you were with me,
You'd whisper, "Have we joined the other
  ghosts?"

Robes

When children had children's bodies at the beach,
They dived in, wagging legs, and turned to wave hello:
"How Do I Look Now?" Not loud enough.
Voices skid under the waves, heave in foam.

The daughter wades in, turning to wave hello.
The father watches when Mother shakes her hair.
Voices skid under, heave in foam:
The daughter shakes her hair and Father laughs.

And Father watches Mother shake her hair.
And they will age; the daughter waiting,
Shaking her hair, and Father laughs.
The shapes they make crack and disappear.

And the daughter will age, waiting
For the body she had, a child's body.
The shape she had may disappear
In water, sounds, holding barnacles on rocks.

When did she have a child's body?
From a distance, women still hear a sucking
Sound, holding them, barnacles on rocks,
Or letting them suck and cuddle and rock.

Distant women still hear a sucking
Sound: Men who touch, who will be touched,
Or let them suck and cuddle and rock.
This is not a conversation for the shore.

The sound of women wanting to touch, be touched.
Children always watch the grown-ups talk.
This is not a conversation for the shore.
Robes will cover what we saw.

Children watching grown-ups talk
Forget their robes. They touch each other's burns.
Robes will cover what we saw.
Father gathers the snapshots he took.

She wants Father's robe. They touch each other's burns.
"How Do I Look Now?" Not loud enough
To call Father back from the snapshots he took
When children had children's bodies at the beach.

A Wild Plum Is for Independence

I

See how she holds the plum
Between fingers less elegant than the gesture,
The inspection in Foodtown
Among the abundance of imported lemons, black
Grapes. See how she weighs
First the shade of violet: looking under queer
Fluorescent light at edges,
Dappling red and purple, that color neither
Blue nor there, like a wine,
A bull's blood, a blue blood, a color reserved
For queens. The sails on
Cleopatra's ships were dyed a certain purple
Like the plum she holds:
Not quite a woman, the transvestite quadroon.

II

I must confess I paused
There between the limes and apples to appraise
Her chest. Skin: Much
Exposed between the borders of a tropical shirt.
And stubble returned. In a glance,
Looked not like hair but nicks healing, a stretch
Of injury between the parrots
Falling, each bird flooding the next one red.

III

When I was called a girl,
They said, "You are too old to run outside
Without a shirt." I was six,
And my brother ran with me under the sprinkler.
High fans of water
Bent to the grass: One half, the other, gentle
As a skeleton of waves.
My brother pulled his shirt off, and water spattered
Him, like teeth grinning,
Wet teeth falling on weeds. My skin tanned quicker,
But only where it showed.

IV

The woman in Foodtown, nestling
Plums in her basket, shows so much skin, and how
Did she choose, or when did it
Seem palpable: There before him, a premonition,
A gift of silk stockings,
Out-of-season lilies . . . or earlier, earlier,
When did it begin—when
Did I—She moves among the dark and light
Apples. She knows what she needs.
And what if I refuse—gather them all
Instead, the orange peaches,
Watermelons, dripping cinnabar
And scarlet juices—suck

Them all, beyond choice. The bitter rubbing
Sugar, waves on a tongue.
No thought, nothing but circles of pink:
The mouth holds the body in place.

V

I could tell her how I slept
With my brother, bathed with him that summer
When nights held the long-
Accumulated heat. We asked for fans,
And noises, beetles
Lost and hitting the screen, faded in a whir,
A lullaby that dulled us.
I could tell her how we slept: The hands
That scratched each other quiet
Quiet now; breathing one another—
Don't make me sleep alone.

VI

And how does she know when it ends?
The transvestite poses in the check-out line,
Deftly studying blush
In a little mirror, as if someone will be there
When she enters with bags, bottles.
He will look first to see how pretty she is.
My brother saw my body

In a soft yellow dress. "You look swell."
I looked away, smiled, afraid
I would arouse him, the way a woman steps back
So that a man may lead.
I waited afternoons in my parents' house,
Moving only to mirrors,
The glass covering colored prints of fruit.
Boys dropped by, and what else
Happened, I don't know, except how I waited.
"Be still and he will find you."
That is what I learned, not to move, and when I did,
I came upon this pause—
As when a plum catches light, and the ineffable
Blue slows the impetus
To move beyond the *choose me, choose me,*
Painted burgundy on lips.

Cameos

Cameos

Rituals of loveliness, bolted to the year,
Change in the shades of pomegranate,
But not in earnest ablution, earnest lotions

And powders in enameled tins. The primping
Of girls enunciates the world at home:
How much is malice; how much prismatic?
A song of protest may improvise

The inarticulate, a cappella:
An anatomy of pornography,
Anatomies of beauty or geometry.

A song of protest may improvise the inarticulate
And play together empty robes and
The marble abdomens of broken goddesses.
Rituals of loveliness begin

With a mother's cologne: An evening canticle
That sweetens childish good-nights, before she leaves
And the door shuts. Laughter

Simmers through the window, wrapped in queer, adult
    opacity.
And there are always mornings on a weekend,
Before the mother's mirror, when her abalone comb
Through the daughter's hair seems a charm

Into the strangeness of the mother's world:
I am a woman as I comb my hair.
And the child's body flaunts

A vanity not her own and her own;
Not her mother's, and yet,
The legends of a woman and her mirror
Tumble from the shelf: Symphonies

Of auburn and barrettes; ringlets and
Gardenias pinned above the nape.
A woman and her mirror: A duet

Of fantasy and power. How much is malice;
How much prismatic? Another song
Would mention Venus: The foam and the hair
Botticelli painted as a flourish on the sky.

A flourish; and the way she had of catching
Strands to hide her genitalia.
A modest Aphrodite, languid, autonomous.

The still shimmering skin is her power.
Though how much is myth; how much custom?
Eve comes more to mind, never shedding
The paradox of regret and thought.

She is only pretty in Eden,
Among apricots and leopards.
The bitter arbors of tomorrow unimagined.

There were mirrors in the garden,
Small reflections after rain and
In the infant lakes that never shivered.
The early years belong to an anatomy

Of beauty: Gold light on a young woman's toes
As she opens the bubbles of lavender fish,
Alone and happy enough that her thoughts measure

The animations of clouds and what she last
Tasted: pears and grapes, chartreuse and blue.
An anatomy of beauty is a woman
Alone or insulated by the steam

Of distance, south seas or a turkish bath,
Where space is littered with soft arms, embraces,
Swirls of ivory and amber light.

Is this paint or a woman? Attitude
Names beauty or pornography,
And a song of protest may include
A loveliness that hesitates between the two.

Such seduction leaves a fear of seduction,
A fear that odalisques and other erotica
Provoke only wishes to possess.

Possess the Ingres' bather, the lavish, indolent back.
Rituals of loveliness, of insolent
Fecundity, come of a woman's first
Duet with her mirror, the mother's mirror.

And in this seclusion of wishes painted on the skin,
A woman dreams her illusions of power.
How much is malice; how much prismatic?

She knows the song of protest in the street
Serenade, where there is only one
Refrain: A hounding into shame, the sham
Of flattery. That is when her body

Is a power: A song of protest
Improvising the inarticulate
Tangle of loveliness and rage.

That is when a power overwhelms—
When the strange hand reaches for a covered breast.
And the mirror cracks across, down,
Making alternate duets:

A song of horror, a song like Eve's regret.
An anatomy of beauty is without regret,
Succinct as the hasty step

Of nudes on a stair. Where do they go?
Painters clip the women to pieces,
Cropped nocturnes, masks and angles.
Figures vaporize in dreams of white

Diagonals. An anatomy of beauty
May include geometry and air.
A song of protest may improvise

An inarticulate revulsion to the rubbing out
Of women. De Kooning and Picasso.
Deformity embraced as part of an affair
Of shapes, cubes—a truth

Replaces rituals of loveliness.
Though within a woman's home,
There will always be a mirror: A duet

Of fantasy and power. How much is malice;
How much prismatic? The woman leaves,
The door shuts, and she hears her own shoe on the stair.
And later she will tell me of the hours

As a model, hours in a pale room with skylights
And eyes that weigh her symmetry with theirs.
"They showed me where to change—behind a screen.

An odd habit, I thought, the note of reserve
In a swarm of scrutiny and dirt.
So I shrugged and stripped by the nearest chair,
Quick as I could, the jeans and cotton stripes.

A perfunctory transition from person to art.
My lover knew I sat for painters.
He was never prudish till I told him that.

And he scowled and said, " 'Beauty is a stillness,
A form examined in repose. Motion
Makes pornography. Inches of skin
Insinuate, no matter the speed.' "

And now we argue this, over Degas' whores
And Rubens' raped daughters. Are these not art;
Are these not titillation: A song of protest

May improvise the inarticulate,
A duet of women afraid of hysteria,
Lured into loving French pastels, chartreuse
And blue, and naming the taken women

Baroque light. An anatomy of beauty
Is more than a nude, more than what a nude
Is doing, posed while semi-artists squint

And fake her silhouette. And when she leaves
And the door shuts, how much beauty
Will divert her stride? The clouds, too fickle
To be snow; the puddles sprung apart

By running children. Confusion in
These lines of flux and physics could make
A history of dissolving thighs

An apt reply. Though when were clouds poised?
When were women ever still as linen?
The song of protest may be a paradox
Of loveliness and rage, a litany of cameos:

I am an artist as I make a mark of haunting.
For the duet of power may remain
A fantasy, a power of surfaces,

Scarlet powders and cloth. An anatomy of beauty
Changes in the shades of pomegranate,
But not in longing for leopards, the man and woman,
Tender in embracing world as much as paint.

Momentum: Waving Back, Turning Away

Ballad Aubade

We lie across embroidered dahlias,
Arms on auburn leaves,
On Dubonnet-colored sheets and afghans
Knit of bluish greens.

What I used to let men do; let them
Pick . . . "Don't tell me,"
You smile, looking at your thumb.
I almost told you secrets

Other lovers had. Or ways
I tried to run away,
Taking off my clothes for money,
Like taking off my body

Or taking from this evening its
Severance from the past,
So kisses distract and substitute
And suffocate the last—

I bring all this to bed with me,
As anecdotes, of course,
Looking at you as though you dream
Heroics, waking before

The shooting starts. Who started it?
Remember winters, we
Stayed wrapped in wool, held in
Pitch like touch repeated.

Love poems flesh out and subdue
Longing; longing as regret.
"Don't bring all that in here with you."
Afraid you'd say it,

But you didn't. You said, "Who'd ever
Want to publish love poems?
Why not give them to the lover,
Or husband, if he's home."

Because I'm still afraid? Because
We were busy laughing,
Before our bodies fell to hushing.
Because love learns

What not to say, as the sun
Separates skin from the sound
Of birds awake, their mouths
Pecking sky, instead of each other.

Tulip Repetition

When tulips were named for mistresses, mountain bliz-
    zards,
Named for parrots and herons;
When tulips opened their virus
Crescents, their lily petals; emphatic amethysts
Arced open, and tulips
Blew apart; the shreds flew
Over fences, alleys, city blocks of steps to the water,
The way they did long ago,
When tulips were named for Darwin,
Named for tales when Little Red was eaten; hundreds
Of reds in public gardens,
Where children would take another,
Another petal, throwing them in fountains; the pastel
Boats would swirl away,
Their parties torn apart
On currents, hisses; water coming down on them
From stone puckers; figures
Leap at one another,
Or did once and were caught. Children ran off,
Plucking more yellow, pink,
Like hands of cupids removed
Finger by finger, as the citronella candles
Joined their cigarettes,
And adults went on murmuring
In their own yards. And only later, when
I could look at them again
And wanted lavenders,
The viridescent hybrids; when the mummied bulbs
Arrived in bubble-pack,

And later turned to blushing
Colors like the summer robes of concubines:
The rustled indigo
With flecks of unripe melon;
When tulips opened in the sun, the petals flared
A salmon-rose, like ears
Burning when your name—
I wanted to tell you when tulips opened—the later
Versions of rouge and pearl—
I wanted you to see them!
Before the wind—before the tulips blew apart—
But then I heard that pulling,
Me pulling that mottled
Apricot, the pink, pulling the petals off tulips,
So you would notice me,
But you weren't even there.
So I ran out to the tulips and heard men come
To the other side of the fence
And clear the scattered trash.
They dozed among the pints of Wild Turkey, and then
Stood like statues, relieving
Themselves behind the cars.
In the garden, I heard the ones with orange caps;
The one holding his arm,
His eyes layered with the work
Of turning what he does to what he knows; and when
He lay down beside the fence,
Didn't he dream Caribbean women held him? For hours
Their bracelets, charms of jade,
Sang, and they covered him

And let him sleep. And later, after dark, when tulips
Closed, I wanted to forget
How often I would ask you
To take me back among the tulips in our yard,
Back through shapes of smoke.
"Are you still sleeping?" you asked.
Your hand buried in my hair. "Don't you smell it?
Come inside." The hospital
Burns its medical waste;
The smoke across the neighborhood; a smell the tulips
Inherit, like citronella,
This vapor of dissected saints.

A Letter

W: (double you). A sound, a gutturally modified
Bilabial voiced spirant. ("Spirant": Fricative.
"Fricative": The forcing breath through constricted . . .)
Woman: sing. *wifman.* sing. *wim(m)on; wyman.*
Sing "a form peculiar to English," after *wife.*
Wife: The ancient word (not the pseudo-etymologic
Woe). sing. *wip.* sing. *viv.* Not Gothic,
But queer how "obscure the origins," from *wife* to

Queen! Quene occasionally found in ME.,
And not an ordinary *wife;* only
"The wife of a king or (in poetry)
A famous person." Who (in poetry)
Is famous? You, if doubled love speaks to you.
A written arousal made in ME. to double you.

Again, I Write You About Tomorrow

Apologizing at the beginning for my ignorance.
I forget what isn't written down, as though
Language were born again a mother scribbling,
"Remember: Wash your hair and wear a coat!"

No, I haven't time to see you this week,
But writing, for a Woman of Letters, saves
The sifting, later, through such mental debris
That we—or I—would pile . . . ; and saves

Me the embarrassment—that stutter—
As you scan my latest, best infirmities.
Thank you for your letters.
I still consider myself the one who listens,

Then laugh, startled by inquiries: You ask
If poetry still has "universal emotional appeal"
In these chaotic days, both vacuous
And overannotated. You do not see,

I hope, poetry as charity,
A refuge for those members of humanity
Who will not dress their wounds! "No one believes,"
You wrote, "that death, love, etc. are shared facts (*sic*).

'My mother suffered so differently from yours,'
Professors concluded at the MLA."
Do you want my disgust as a restorative?
A Woman of Letters, admittedly addlepated

In sensible shoes, may refer to herself
In the third person, as though she dwells among
The untrodden thinkers of another century,
Perfecting the apology, her chosen song.

A barking form. Excuse me. Excuse me,
A ululation, like a lullaby,
Crooned across the many rivers, in Vietnamese.
A shushing sound I still admire,

But you've read my monographs on that.
Did I apologize for never answering
Your other letter? I helped establish
Another library for battered women.

"It all happened so rapidly, by chance,"
I told reporters, so as not to appear
Immodest. You wrote me that, perhaps,
Women no longer bend to dreary

Blushes; no longer speak of themselves
As canaries; broken doves; no longer
Beauty as a prerequisite to being held—
Heard. I meant to say, heard.

I meant to tell you what I learned,
Fielding questions with a brief report
On the days we bound ourselves, furiously,
In bandages to end the war.

We came alive in anger, improvising
Chants; slogans; banners. Not poetry,
But words, like pieces of brain, spilled, and I
Gasped, when hundreds of mouths screamed

The earnest jingles I invented: "War:
A wealth of death to help the wealthy live."
Or was it, "Let the wealthy bore
Themselves to death"? Both anachronistic

Now. Now what seems most "universal" is
Apocalyptic, but, as you wrote so deftly,
"If snow is an endangered species, is it
Poetry?" Enlarging definitions

Will never save poetry from extinction
Or save the planet. Yes, for years, I
Lived near the river, translating lyrics
Of annihilated tribes.

Phrases turn the open sores to bodies
Healing themselves with flesh and sleep.
Lungs take in smoke and the faded
Breath of dead coyotes. Words leave

The tongue: "Never before seen": Repeated:
"Never seen again": Medicine was poetry, but
Herbs are more romantic than surgery.
They said I was afraid. Wrong. Skulls

Exhumed and buried again among their own:
That is all they wanted. I saw too much.
The water resource specialists and homes
For runaways. The years I watched

The river change from shoe-color to
Another long infection. Why are you happy
I was there? Was the world improved
The day I summarized how unfashionable

The tribal crisis was: No picturesque criminals.
My journal stammered unattractively: "I, I." I joined
The Choked Whisper School of Poetry for Women.
A woman's suffering, I know,

Becomes archaic, and you slip away, diverted,
Then ensconced, in your own age. Remember
When I showed you my mother's grandmother's
Pillows, stitched from her sons' handkerchiefs?

"I wanted to forget the bodies of my children,"
She said. "Dead and—" So different,
As you say, from what I know. My children
Never lay under the bodies of soldiers waiting to die.

I remember my mother pressed her hands on her chest,
Turning away. She had told me her wounds: "This
Skin" on her chest breaking open; then
What could she "put there" to stop the—"Listen,

Don't listen. Don't look at me." She turned away.
Did I remind you how useful it is to declare
Your writing true? Let your voice break:
The horror, horror, harrowing:

How language cannot contain the wounds. Note
The universal appeal made specific
In the first person ("How I suffered; oh—").
The syntax breaks (Proof!)—implicit

Agony secures the TV-movie of your life.
What has more "emotional appeal" than that?
Your words in the mouths of stars who die,
Bleeding in oval shapes. The actors

Rarely die to make finales realistic.
You should ask if I enacted pain to—write,
Calling myself the victim-witness-priestess
Who knows she dies—is dying

Imperceptibly, her hand warmed by remote
Controls, switching channels. She controls
The news, cartoons. The nurse said, "Her only
Exercise is argument," pointing

To my mother. I watched her change the channels.
TV lions paw into the—evening news:
The weather cloudy; winds from Canada.
The stars still dance through midnight movies.

This is not what you asked. A Woman of Letters
May remain perplexed that age provides nothing,
Nothing but refrains: Remember when;
Remember me. Memories, like tourniquets, numb

An audience. So this is where I stop
And read this letter, where I would erase
All but the answers to your appropriate
Questions, making the page a white face

With nothing there but wise conclusions.
If later you receive some cryptic syllables,
Oracular, instead of this, I want you
To throw them out and call, until

I admit the life you asked about—what
Happened to the days, the work, the woman
Who made apologies her poetry because
She was afraid? Or angry; both. Watch

The hours I never touch fall in a wake behind me.
You asked me to remember; no.
It's your turn. I came this far—didn't mean
To do what I did; didn't know

How much silence held me. Held thought,
Like chiseled bowls, warmed and held for wine,
Like anthropology invented as a hobby
By the rich. How much silence

I associate with pain. You know, the formal
Feeling. Oh yes, the stapled cummerbund
And pearls sewn to ample breasts. Orders
To close her lips; close eyes. And come

Into the mystery we filigree on ignorance.
Now you do it. Your turn. Take the words,
Confetti for the world. Take the world,
Take rivers, the language we threw:

Susquehanna, Colorado, then Cytoxin, antibodies
Dumped and mixed to incantations. Evenings
We repeated, "It won't hurt at all." The needles,
Tubes of blood, chilled for each disease.

Listen. Don't listen. Among stars,
We shrink to flecks of steam, fast evaporating:
What I am doing—a cloudy dot, far
Away. Don't turn away, before

You learn more than I did: More than brief
Accompaniments: O come to me and comfort me.

Song of Many Pauses

A windy sunlight fans the slender laurel wings,
The layered fans of ginkgo leaves,

This yellow serenade:
The low staccatos of yellow birds.

"Bright colors are happy colors," the children yell,
As they run into the woods to play.

Watch the henna-color, burnt sienna,
Speckled, freckled, foxed, flocked,

The maple, birch, the severed chilly flocks.
Melodies emanate from refrain

And what may be sustained,
And will I hold on to this:

A shuttle of red and yellow
Finger shapes, now eyes, now ruined teeth?

Where are the mouths for every mouth?
The ash leaves look like open mouths.

The mountain ash, the weeping
Willow-leaved pear. Look there,

Not at more wishes on my tongue
Like those of children, whirling themselves

And laughing at anything, even wishes,
Wishes, like this one, to stop.

Notes

"Untitled": Line 6 is taken from *The American Heritage Dictionary*'s definition of the "dawn redwood."

"Fragments of an Eve": Poem III refers, in part, to the following: "Usually [the newborn baby] can make such consonants as *m, w, y, g, r* and *h;* and the vowels found in the words *see, pat, father, pool* and *how.*" *The Mother's Encyclopedia* (New York: The Parents' Institute, 1949), vol. 6, p. 1188.

"Fragments of an Eve": Poem VIII notes, with regard to the starfish: "Wrapping its arms over a clam, the starfish uses sustained suction of the tube feet to force it open. Then it extends its stomach through its mouth into the clam shell and digests the clam there." Herbert S. Zim and Lester Ingle, *Seashores* (New York: Simon & Schuster, 1955), p. 63.

"Pictures of an Exhibition": Lines are borrowed from Eugene Mirabelli's "Looking and Not Looking: Pornographic and Nude Photography," *Grand Street* 5, no. 1 (1985): 207–8.

> the erotic power in the image of an unclothed body is greater in a literal photograph than in a similar painting, because the painting is inevitably to some degree an idealization . . . anything that comes between the image and the viewer will suggest artifice and reduce the erotic strength of the image.

"Her Epithalamium": Lines allude to the following passage from Joseph T. Shipley's *Dictionary of Word Origins* (Paterson, N.J.: Littlefield, Adams & Co., 1961), p. 160.

OE. *leaf,* permission; by your *leave.* (*Leave,* as trees in
spring, is from ME. *leve* from *lef, leaf.*) This is related
to *lief,* from AS. *leof,* dear, a common Teut. word;
Goth. *liufs;* L. *lubet,* it delights; AS. *lufu,* whence Eng.
love. Sansk. *lubh,* to desire . . . But note that what we
like, we think is just so; hence, OHG. *gilouban;* AS.
geliefan, whence ME. *beleven,* whence Eng. *believe.*
Thus we *believe* in what we love.

"Postcard of Degas' *Washerwomen Carrying Washing*":
Lines refer to Catherine Beecher's *A Treatise on Domestic
Economy* (1841; reprint, New York: Schocken Books,
1977), pp. 314–15: "the grease should be removed . . . by
French chalk . . . Then wash and rinse in the hay-water,
stiffening with glue-water."

"Cameos": The paintings by Degas of women bathing use
ritualized poses of seduction common among prostitutes
in the nineteenth century.